DEARLOGUE
POETIC DUET IN LANGUAGE OF LOVE

DEARLOGUE
POETIC DUET IN LANGUAGE OF LOVE

Abubakar Othman

&

Habeebatu X!

Malthouse Press Limited

Lagos, Benin, Ibadan, Jos, Port-Harcourt, Zaria

© Abubakar Othman and Habeebatu X! 2020
First Published 2020
ISBN: 978-978-58297-4-7

Published in Nigeria by

Malthouse Press Limited
43 Onitana Street, Off Stadium Hotel Road,
Off Western Avenue, Lagos Mainland
E-mail: malthouselagos@gmail.com
Facebook:@malthouselagos
Twitter:@malthouselagos
Istagram:@malthouselagos
Tel: 0802 600 3203

Distributors:
African Books Collective Ltd, Oxford, UK
Email: abc@africanbookscollective.com
Website: http://www.africanbookscollective.com

DEDICATION

To:

Ismaila Bala Garba for providing the link,
Naseeba Babale for putting in a word,
Khalid Imam for starting it all.
And the All Poets Network for holding on.
We love you all.

ACKNOWLEDGEMENTS

We gratefully acknowledge the contributions of Bala I. Garba and Poetic Wednesday for the Interview Segment of this book, and Professor Idris Amali for recognizing the expedience of this dearlogue.

You are the forbidden lines
In the poetry I was never
Supposed to read...
And I am the unrepentant sinner
Reading your lines.

- *Naseeba Babale*

CONTENTS

PROLOGUE

We're two scores, the decades between us
Two cities far off, the distance in-between us
But this dearlogue, my dear love
Defies time, defies space.

The decades dividing us
Is just the distance between our lips
Lying, heart close to heart
Listening, to the audible silence of our hearts.

This dearlogue defies all gravity
Leaps all virtual bounds
To define us with the intricate simplicity
Of our language of love.

-Othman/Habeebatu

Habeebatu X!

IF THEY ASK ME …

Who is YOU
They would ask ME
Of you

Beloved, I'd tell them
That –

You are ME before time
You are my pride
You are the birthmark adorning
My bounteous chest

Until –
YOU kissed ME
And YOU morphed into ME
Blurring the lines between
YOU and ME
And now
ME is YOU

So if they ask ME of YOU
I'd tell them to search for
YOU in ME
Trace you to ME
Find YOU with ME

There is no WE nor US
Just YOU that is ME
And ME that is YOU

2

Our complex pronoun,
The poetic licence of
Our language of love

Abubakar Othman

TELL THEM

Who is ME
They would ask YOU
About ME

Tell them, my beloved
That –

ME is my name
ME is my personal pronoun
No one calls me by it but ME

ME is myself
ME is my personal property
ME is my identity
Until the day I met YOU,
And they saw ME
Kissing YOU,
They now refer to ME as YOU

ME and YOU
A conjugal conjunction,
ME now WE
Lying legs up
In the poetic ecstasy
Of platonic love

Habeebatu X!

IF NOT FOR US ...

If not for us
The words wouldn't exist,
What purpose would they serve
Other than to pick the honeydew from my lips
And settle them on your tongue
Like the morning aurora from my lake
Peeping into the upper atmosphere of your legs

If not for us
Poetry would never have been
What purpose would it serve
But to be a furnace
Of burning passion
That melts me like gold
Coating every inch of you
Seeping into your veins
Making wild love to your arteries

Gently, gently, my beloved
We are just beginning
The stroke burns
Like the caress of the sun,
We are an infinity wrapped in eternity
We are the figurative language of love
Wrapped in metaphysical metaphors
Sealed with sinful similes
Hidden in hedonistic hyperboles,

If not for us, my love
Poetry shall be picked
From the bellies of termites

Abubakar Othman

IF NOT FOR POETRY

If not for poetry
How would I have kissed you,
The taste of your tongue
Still lingers in my mouth

Tongue to tongue
You left erotonic taste in my mouth
And now like a drop of phillthre
Down the right ventricle of my heart
You set the blood circulation aflame

Softly, softly, my beloved
I know the firm breasts
Are soft enough for the embrace,
And the nipples that nibble my heart
Dispense eroyonic desires,
But this love, my beloved
Must last beyond
These lines of poetry

Habeebatu X!

EVERYTHING

If passion is what sets your heart aflame
Then poetry is my passion
For my heart now lay in ashes.

If love is what gives your eyes that twinkle
Then poetry is my love
For she has hidden stars in my eyes.

If obsession is what dominates your thoughts
Then poetry is my obsession
For she sits regally in my mind.

If addiction is what gives you cravings
Then poetry is my addiction
For she is that which I cannot do without

If lust is what makes you drop your clothes
Then poetry is my lust
For she makes me drop even my skin for her

If everything is what makes me who I am
Then poetry is my everything
For what am I, if not rhymes, verses and YOU.

Abubakar Othman

EVERYTHING IS ME

If poetry is your everything
Then everything is me
For I'm the poet with
The cardiovascular verses
For the rhymes and rhythms
Of your heartbeats.

If poetry is what makes you
Drop your clothes like slough
Then I'm the poet with
The lustful fingers on your waist
To make you drop even your skin
For me.

If poetry is your addiction
That gives you the insatiable cravings
Then I'm the poet with the addictive voice
That dominates your thoughts
With lustful passions.

If poetry is your love
Then, my beloved
I'm the poet that sees
Sensuous imagery in your eyes
Tantalizing metaphors in your words
Striking similes in your smiles
That leave me with dangling modifiers
In my eyes.

Habeebatu X!

YOU DESECRATED MY HOLY GROUND

You crawled into my Temple
With head hung low
Kissing the prints my feet left
On exotic beaches and jungle paths

You begged for salvation
And merciful goddess I am,
I guided your hands through
The contours of my scripture
Melded to my skin like birthmark
And gave you faith

When you transgressed, sinner that you are
You found penance in the rosary beads
Hanging from my waist, stroking till you're pleased

You came to me, a pervert lost in yourself
A cast off at sea with no present, no future
You knelt before my altar, a penitent
Crying and pleading –
And goddess that I am
I opened your eyes to my bounties
Cast you on the waves of my upsurge
And let you flow to a relief

And when you hungered, I fed you
And when you thirsted, you drank
From my watering hole, gulping in haste,
You came to me, a liar hidden in penury

And when I gave from my riches
You swore by the secrets hidden in my eyes
To be devout, placing your hands on my sacred spaces
You pledged life, death and life after to worship me.

You drank of my communion for immortality
Then graced your heart and declared
Yourself god, knocked down my Temple like dominos
And desecrated my holy ground.

Abubakar Othman

THE MERCIFUL GODDESS

My goddess, you lured me
Into the sacred thickets of your Temple
Tempted me with scabrous gestures
I, a penitent acolyte in spiritual penury
Standing sentinel at the gate of your holy ground

I sought salvation in your scriptures
But you led my eyes to your striptease
Urging me with erotic dentures
To embrace the new faith
Strewn on the rosary beads
Hanging from your waist

We knelt together at your altar
Knees kneading knees
Needing each other
And the merciful goddess that you are
You offered yourself for the sacrifice
And gave me dominion over your altar
Oh! most merciful goddess.

When I hungered, I feasted on the altar
When I thirsted, I gulped from the altar
There is nothing sinful in living off
A merciful goddess.
I demolished the Temple
To erect in our eyes a phalicoyonic edifice
For our worshipful indulgence
My pledged love, our sacred secret.

Habeebatu X!

YOURS ...

Wandering hands rampaging my heart,
Yours.
Like a kid licking licorice – sticky
Fingers fiddling with my heart, leaving bruises
Throwing the wrapper away with tantrums
And still my heart beats,
Yours.
Even when you break the candy too hard
Gobbling the grains greedily
Like pigeons pecking about
Digging their sharp talons into my heart,
Yours

Yours –
My heart that is licorice, candy, grain
To devour with the hunger of a thousand
Starving men – yours.

Abubakar Othman

AND YOURS ...

A yodelling voice caressing my heart,
Yours.
A cool tongue licking my ear,
Yours.
Fast fingers foraging the furs of my chest,
Yours.

And what is 'yours' without 'y' is ours,
Ours.

Yours licorice is ours local rice
And yours to devour,
Me, I, myself
Lisping on your lips.

Habeebatu X!

OF LOUD MUSIC

These days, I dance a lot
Off beat – really hard
To music only I can hear
Of hearts cracking like ice
Meeting the swift kiss of a pick
Still I dance – really bad.

And I sing
At the top of my voice
Off key – really loud
To notes only I can hear
Of hearts crying like flies
Trapped in a moving car
Still I sing – really bad.

I can't dance, I can't sing
Yet still I do, to make up
For the truth –
I can't love another
I can't love no other!

Abubakar Othman

NOT EVERY MUSIC THE FEET CAN DANCE

Not every music the feet can dance
Some drums throb for the heart
And many a good dancer
Dances off beat – really out of sync,
Where the lame leads the agile
As the master dancer
On the tympanic membrane
Of the drum.

Is not every song the heart can sing
Some lyrics have their melodies
In the volcanic waves of the blood
Which only the lonely knows, like
The silent notes of the concerto
Sang off key by the *inamorata*
Who closed off on his *inamorato*

Habeebatu X!

A BITE OF THE SUN

Let's leap together
Hand in hand
For a bite of the sun
You and me
Defying gravity

Abubakar Othman

A SEASON IN THE SUN

This season in the sun
Gives me dizzying delight,
Floating out of gravity
You and I, flirting
In the clouds
Free from cares

Habeebatu X!

MY FIRST SIGHT OF YOU

My first sight of you
Made me like one blinded
By the absoluteness of light,
My retina clawed at the eyes
Blocking every other image
Apart from you taking me to
A climactic height.

At the grace of your eyes
Everything fell with soft thuds
To the lush green of your lawn
Even me by God, I fell like acorns
Thrust from firs lining a mountain top

At the glimpse of your glistening face
I was eclipsed, like the solar force
Over the lunar face, your shadow
Fell on my sun and the light I hoarded
In my soul flickered, flickered and died out.

Abubakar Othman

BE NOT VISIBLE WITH BEAUTY

An open beauty is to prurient eyes
What an open meat is to insolent flies,
A special delight of the connoisseur
Becomes a lustful diet for the voyeur

It's allure lies not in its looks
It's lure lies most in its taste

Like the open meat
Vultures hover around it

Like the open meat
Flies fiddle with it

And men feast on it
Relishing it, ravaging it

An open beauty
Lies not in the eyes of the beholder
An open beauty lies most
In the mind of the beholder

Habeebatu X!

DON'T...

Don't tell me how you'd love me,
Love me!
The sun spends all day serenading
But runs away when the moon shows up.

Don't be my sun, or moon
Be the sky, regardless of time
It's always there over me.

Don't hide me in your lust vaults,
Flount me!
The flower blossoms all day
And falls away at the touch of the moon,
Don't be my flower, or the petals
Be the stem, regardless of time
It remains green in my heart.

Don't, please don't
Just don't
But all day – be present

Abubakar Othman

DON'T SAY NO

When the pawpaw plant grows
Beyond the embrace of the cuddling wall
Goats can no longer be kept away
By latched gates of the compound.

The season is ripe on your chest
The buds burst in florets of fancy
And bees can no longer be kept away
From the fragrant nectar of your season.

The dwarf walls cuddling your waist
The green bracts of your branches
Swaying seductively above the walls,
Here I squat beneath the wall
Beneath your swaying palms
Beckoning, waiting for an embrace

Do not say no, my green paw-paw
Let your swaying palms taste
The pollen grains of my lips
Don't say no, my love
These burstling buds
Must not wait
     Not wait
         Not wait
No more

Habeebatu X!

STORIES FROM OUR PAST

I don't know how you did it
Infiltrated my heart and corrupted it,
When I was with you, nothing mattered
Not the rules, not my morals, not anything –
All that mattered was you, me, us –
Us together

It didn't matter that everything stopped
When we stepped out of the room,
And it didn't matter either, that
Whenever our lips met
I could taste her goodbye kiss.

II
And sometimes, you watched me
Just being me; so intently and intensely
That I forgot how to fill my lungs with air
How to make my heart plump with blood
How to make my brain think with reason
How to even be me,
Because moments like that
I forgot to be my self
I was simply 'yours'

III
It wasn't something you said
             or something you did
It was the way you crashed into my universe

And became the earth, the flowers, the rivers,
I could not look up
And not be reminded of you.

In the beauty of the sun, the moon and the stars
I cannot escape your invisible presence
By ducking my head
In the way you became
The air around me.

So as long as I live
I feel you filling me
Inside me, around me
All over me
Everywhere...

                    IV
May be in a past life
I was loved so beautifully
By a lover that I carry that love
In my heart.
May be he got me so drunk
On a brew of rum and philter gin
That for a thousand life times, *ad infinitum*
I'd always thirst for that distiller's delight
He filtered down my throat
As he kissed me

Or may be, he bound me with a spell
A hex, a curse, an enchantment
For all the time he whispered
My name as his beloved,

And his tears dropped on my skin
Sinking deep into my soul
That since then, now and forever
His tears shall flow in me as my blood
Or have you forgotten our past, my beloved?

Abubakar Othman

HOW CAN I FORGET THE PAST

I
The present may seem pleasant
But it's just a *deja vu*, a strong nostalgia
For the stories of our past.
History sometimes happens in a jiffy
But the memories last for eternity
There is no moment too brief for memory

How can I forget the stories of our past
Stories of our love
                    Of our lust
                         Our longings ...
Plunging deep down into us,
Us together.

How can I forget that day
You walked into my world with gaiety
Enlivened my heart with poetry
Opened my mind to all possibilities
Made my heartbeats faster than time,
And I found myself crouched
Before your shrine
In a timeless zone of love
Where all I knew was you
Where all I needed was you.

How can I forget the day
We broke your inkpot on impulse
And spilled the red content
On the parchment of my skin –
The most memorable story of our past.

                    II
I Remember the night
The ring tone of my cellphone woke me
With a text message at bedtime
Just after rain,
Reminding me of our tryst in the rain

I scrolled the screen to messages
And pressed on the message to listen
Bu only a silent voice came up
Telling me:
                    Today is 06 – 06 – 06
                    A unique day that will never
                    Come our way again

And the voice faded back
Into the blue light of the cellphone,
Leaving me pondering, wondering
Over these mathemagic figures of love.

I fiddled with the figures in geometric progression
06 + 06 + 06 = 18
Ah! revelation dawn on me:
This geometric equation means
You, my figure 8
And I, your onerous partner

How can I forget that night
You came to me through the cellphone
And how we taught the world
The geometrics of love
Sans kama sutra:
06 – 06 – 06 ...

Yes, 06 was Tuesday
The 06th month of
The 06th year of
The new millennium.
I remember our tryst that day
Playing scramble all day
And how the rain danced around us
Forcing me to a game of R-A-I-N
On a double word score,
And there you were
In the geometric figure 8.

And when you added your B(eauty)
To the R-A-I-N
And used your B-R-A-I-N
To lay down in a game of B-E-D
Placing your irresistible D(esire)
On a double letter score
Again I found your geometric figure 8
In B-E-D

And with the passions of cupid
I laid my S(elf) beside you in the BED
And played the bed game with E(ase)
Ending in a double letter box
Where I placed my X(citement) of the game.

Oh! how can I forget this story of our past.

III

The stories are now past
We are just playing the game on extra time
And baby, I've got to win

The whistle will soon be gone
And face to face before the fans
Our love will face the penalty
And baby, I've got to win.

You dribbled me silly
With your sly styles
Your wiles and guiles
Teasing my balls.
I tried to penetrate you with a long shot
But your magical mien
Stood sentinel at the post
And baby, I've got to win.

I tried you from a corner kick
But your allure lured me off line,
You gave me a pleasant back kick
And I returned a head-kick to your hand
And now the whistle has gone for a foul
I must take the penalty kick
And baby, I've got to win

I won the game at extra cost
But the medal is just for keeps
Our love is but a platonic affair
The fanciful stories of our past.

Habeebatu X!

TOUCH ME

Whenever you touch me
I am in shock – electrocuted,
100000 watts course through my veins
Heating up my red blood cells
Filling me up with your current.

Filling me up with your power
Stirring all my senses,
100000 watts knock my head
I am electrocuted – in shock
Whenever you touch me.

Whenever you touch me
The earth and her 7 cousins
Cease to exist – all I have is
You, you, you and
               You, you, you ...
Orbiting my milky way.

Birthing nebulae in my sky
You, you, you and
               You, you, you ...
Are all I have existing
Nothing else ...
Whenever you touch me.

Abubakar Othman

CAN'T WAIT TO TOUCH YOU

Touch me ...?
What a creamy cup of coffee for me
I'll be sipping this poem all day
You'll feel the electrocution
Of my touch tonight.

Can't wait
          Can't wait
                    Can't wait!
The flow of the electrons through
The aphrodisiac cup, like conductor
Electrifies me:

Feeling it, seeping into me
Feeling it, zipping me down
Feeling it, heating me up
Hot enough to electrocute you.

There will be Xcessiveviolence tonight
And in its X!clamatory thrusts and twists
Plenty of Xhilaration and
Delirious Xhaustion.

Habeebatu X!

YET AGAIN

Heartbroken –

Is not the boy whose prom date
Didn't show up eventually,
It's the tears of a wife whose panties
Are stained red
Yet again.

Heartbroken –

Is not the girl whose boyfriend
Kissed another girl,
It's the groaning of a mother
Whose foetus now lies in dots
Yet again.

Heartbroken –

Is not the bride left standing
At the alter, besotted,
It is the mother of the bride
Abandoned on the dance train.
Yet again.

Heartbroken –

Is not the failure to honour 'I love you'
It's the nightmare of the woman
Whose body has failed to gift her
A child
Yet again.

Abubakar Othman

HEARTBROKEN

I need a cardiac surgeon
With concrete nails for hypodermic needles
Heavy hammers for syringes
And wild claws for gloves
To mend my broken heart.

My cardiac surgeon
Unspiral the cochlea of my ear
Fix its cable to the malleus of your ear
Use it as stethoscope and listen
To the seismic tremor of my broken heart.

My cardiac surgeon
You must use the brail for brain
And feel the empty holes for alphabets
To read the cardiovascular verses
Of my broken heart

When the auscultation is done
And the dissection is to begin
Start from the left ventricle of the heart
To block the blood from returning
To this broken heart.

Habeebatu X!

SOMEWHERE ALONG LOVING YOU

I was
Somewhere along loving you
But I had ceased to exist
I had become this being, this thing
That existed only in the span of your gaze
In the breadth of your tongue.

I was
But only as your eyes besotted me
Only as your hands felt me
And still I wasn't scared, I was willing
To lose myself in the after thoughts of you
To be this thing that lived
To complement you
In this forgettable way.

I was
Somewhere along loving you, needing you
And when you tired, I was willing
To become this ghost, this phantom
Who breathed life into your shell,
Plucking desperately on wayward gazes
And stolen kisses
I wasn't greedy,
I just was
Just was
Was ... X!

Abubakar Othman

AFTER THOUGHTS ARE SWEETER

Sometimes what was enjoyable to do
Comes off sweeter to remember
Like the after thought of us together
Defying gravity.

Somewhere along loving you
I remember with relish
The day I hung on a cliff
Somewhere in the space between your eyes
Defying vision, cuddling you
In optical illusion

And when I became visible
And you in all places pliable
You begged and begged
For a return to after thought
Hanging on a cliff
Loving you.

Habeebatu X!

IF ...

I would fall madly into your arms
If –
You smell like ink on white parchment
And spend mornings with you sipping coffee
Watching the rays of sun make love
To the yellow wings of birds

I would plunge headlong into your arms
If –
You can touch me softly like my muse
Pulling sleep off my eyes and
Replace the madness of words
With the soft sigh of your name

I would fall with zest into your arms
If –
You become my celestial metaphors –
The sun, the moon, the stars,
The flowers, the bees ...
Filling me wholly with similes
Stretching me into a million hyperboles

I would fall with aplomb into your arms
If –
You lead my heart to a museum of poetry
With its mosaic colours of love,
I would fall fully in love with you
If –

And only if,
Poetry makes no sense when
I am in your arms.

Abubakar Othman

ADD LOVE

And to all these qualities,
As would do the Colossians,
Add love.
        That which
              No madly fall
                    No headlong plunge
                         No insatiable zest
But binds them all in perfect harmony
With the celestial melodies
And the telluric rhythms
Of our throbbing hearts;
              That makes poetry paltry
              To satiate our wild desire
              When you are in my arms.

SHOOTING STARS AT 4 A.M.

You would have me lying in bed
At 4 a.m counting the stars
Dotting my ceiling
To how many times you said
'I love you'
And I have lost count
1 star, 3 stars, 455 stars
17,000 stars, 1.3 million stars?

You would have me chasing shooting stars
Blurred by the rain in my eyes
Desperately making wishes
Never heard, never granted
Till I lose count of how many wishes
I have sent, pleading
'Please don't leave me'.

Without you, all I have are
Shooting stars on my skylike ceiling

Abubakar Othman

THE SWEET VOICE AT 4 A.M

The sweet sonorous voice from the minaret
Comes tearing through to my heart at 4 a.m
Like the shooting stars in the night
Brightening the dark sky,
                Calling me to devotion
                  Hayyalalsalat!
                    Hayyalalfalaa!

I must rise to this call
The first call of the five chores
When the dawn is falling down
Over a dull slumbering town.

But this succubus glued to my bosom
Shooting soothing stars
Into my inchoate heart
Weighs me down with another call
Telling me at 4 a.m.
                'Please don't leave me
                Without you all I have are shooting
stars ...
              1 star, 3 stars, 455 stars, 17,000 stars
              1.3 million stars ...'
The rhythmic voice of her heartbeat
Mixes with the distant voice of the minaret
In the audio-sensuous ears of my heart
And they got me lost in the conflicting calls
Coming like shooting stars at 4 a.m.

Habeebatu X!

YOU ENSNARED ME

Where once I thought it would feel like dying
It now feels like wanting to die
Yet knowing this heart has a million beats
And so it beats
         and beats
              and beats ...
Till the mysteries unravel like blood
Whispering the horrors of a split artery.

You taught me that hearts don't break
At least not beautifully as in art and poetry
Of course mine doesn't –
It tugs at its seams
         and pulls
             and pulls
                  and pulls ...
Till the wonders of the iroko roots
Are laid bare to the elders of the wind.

Where once I thought I loved you
Life has taught me love is not enough
We are not fairy tales, we're not magic
There is simply no 'we'
But you I love
         and love
             and love
Till the word loses all meaning
And all meanings are lost
And still you I love.

Abubakar Othman

LOVE ...

If not for you
This word long departed
Would not woo me back to its folds
Thirsting
        Trusting
Tasting once more
The softness of your lips.

Forlorn for long
Silence serves me solace
In the inaudible serenade
Of your absence
Lisping in my ears.

To taste love again
The erotonic pill for pain
Spread on your yonic lips
Like the icing on the cake
Gives me respite from pining
That feels like wanting to die.

If not for you
I'd have broken to a million pieces
Dejected. Rejected. Neglected.

Habeebatu X!

TEACH ME

I've fallen carelessly in love
With you and your bewitching spell
So hard, so careless
I've hit my head rock-bottom in your heart.

In your heart I'm a stranger
I don't know you, I don't know my self
I know nothing no more but
This feeling that fills my heart,
Beclouds my vision
                     Seeing nothing
                         Thinking nothing
                             But you.
So teach me, how to love you
I'm eager to please you, to love you
Hold my hands and guide my feet
Through the contours of your heart,
Hold me steady as I stretch up
To pluck the stars off the sky
To adorn you in celestial splendour.

Hold me tightly by the thighs
As I reach for the monsoon moon
To tap its wet torrents of love
To wet your insatiable desire,
Hold me tightly by the waist
As I reach to the sun to tap its current
To caress your sovereign body.

Hold me to your heart, tightly, tightly
So the winds do not scatter me away
Like pollen off your petals
Hide me securely like the nectar
Of your phallic vault

My love, please
Teach me how to love you
So I may never forget.

Abubakar Othman

TEACH YOU?

Haba! **Yahabibi**,
What else is there to teach you about love
You, whose name personifies it
You, the armourous conqueror of my heart
You, the unmatchable goddess of beauty
You, whose fu-x!-king fire burnt to ashes
The great pyramids of Kano.

My merciful goddess
What can I teach you about the depth of love
You who plunged deeper than the diver
Into the cosy sea of my heart
Reaching rock-bottom with aplomb.

The goddess of the river is no stranger
In the kingdom of the sea, you're welcome
My heart is now your Queendom.
Tonight the fresh water of your river
Shall taste the salty water of my sea
Filling us with feelings
Only us together feel.

Heroine of my heart
What can I teach you about height in love
You who reached higher than the Astronaut
Into the celestial space of fantasy
Plucking love and splendour from the clouds
To adorn and adore my sovereign body.

In the depth of my heart
We defy gravity to gravitate freely
In the luscious waves of our
Fresh and salty waters
Gliding giddily
        Thighs to thighs
            Waist to waist
                Chest to chest
Hitting your head against the rock-bottom
Of my heart.

Habeebatu X!

I'M FIRE

I'm not meant to be hidden
In the flimsy lines of your poetry
My flame ensnared by your metaphors
My smouldering fires smothered by your hyperboles
I would burn them all.

Every word used to woo me
Would scatter like sand grains
In the desert after a storm
Every word about me would melt
Like iceberg being kissed by the sun
I would burn them all.

I'm not meant to be tucked away
Into the lustfulness of your static stanzas
My fiery red burns brighter than
What your ogling eyes can tame
I would burn them to ashes.

My fire, by God! My fire
Has the sun peeking through the clouds
Envious of this being that
Overshadows its shadow
Hanging by the threads of light
I cast on its orbit.

My fierce fires frightened him
And he knows for sure

I would burn him to ashes
Till he drops like snowflakes
To the ground

Blinded by the dazzling beauty of me
The moon would go to snooze in the dark sky
With her panties wetter than the Amazon rivers
Whispering to the stars about
This fire she has never seen before,
This hot blazing ball of beauty
The red haze of me.

I'm fire! The infernal inferno of love
The incendiary heart of poetry
The inextinguishable flame of beauty,
Your arms cant hold me
I'm not meant to be held by
Unsure hands and unsteady fingers.
I would burn you and him and her
And every one who dares
To put me in a box
So tell them, I'm an erupting volcano
Too hot for the bellies of the mountains
Clawing at their throats till they
Vomit me in spurts of flowing dragons
Fictional, beyond the grasp of reality
I'm a natural disaster
                    Breaking hearts
                            Wrecking havocs
                                    Causing trouble
I'm a fucking fire at your backyard.

Abubakar Othman

BURN THEM

You're a raging fire in the heart of the sea
If the element cannot eliminate you
Who else can dare you,
Burn them!

You're the fire engulfing the fireman's house
If the Extinguisher cannot extinguish you
Who else has the speel to quell you,
Burn them!

You're the wild fire devouring
The forests and cities of the West
If their advanced technologies cannot tackle you
Who else can attack you,
Burn them!

You're the legendry Helene of Troy
Whose face launched a thousand ships of suitors
Whose beauty burnt the topless towers of Illium
Whose sedative kiss gave immortality to men,
But was she not put in Pandora's box and banned
By men insaned by her beauty,
Burn them!

Burn them all
Who dare to stare at your flare
Your beauty is not for prurient eyes,
Not even the elements above
Can hold you at ample view.

Show them the goddess you are
Tempt them with your seductive beauty
And when they come close
Tame them with your fire
Burn them all
My love is enough to last you for eternity.

Habeebatu X!

MOMENTS FOR EVER

I do not promise you tomorrow
Or a decade or forever together
Till death do us part
Time holds no value to me.

But I promise you this, my beloved
For as long as my heart beats
Think in tandem with me that
My heart beats for you
And the blood in my veins
Sing for you as they course

I'd show you love
Better than what the clouds show
When they weep and cry
Shedding profuse tears
For the seedlings to grow.

I'd show you love
Better than the river bank does
When it embraces the cold crash of sea
With the warm arms of earth.

I'd show you love
In this time
In this moment
That makes forever too near
That, my beloved
I promise you.

Abubakar Othman

THE LOVE OF CARROT

The carrot
The root of all fruits,
The carrot the fruit
For all seasons.

The carrot
The fruit only men grow.

The carrot is my garment
Every man has his size
The carrot is my armour
Every man has his weapon.

> The carrot
> Palatable but not edible
> Sweet but not sumptuous
> Pliable but not breakable.

My pen (is) my carrot
Every man has his colour,
My carrot is my pride
Every man has his praise.

My carrot is my prowess
Every man has his stamina
My carrot is my identity
Every man has his skill.

But the pride, prowess and praise
The carrot gets not without you,
Without you my carrot is like
A snail cocooned in its shell.

MADNESS

Beloved, they call me mad
That I have fallen into the traps of poetry
And left my cup of sanity with
Last night's hangover of love.

They say I'm the madness
Filled in the glass of wine
For I'm inebriated in the presence
Of your absence.

They call me a fanatic of love
That I've denounced religion
To worship you with the ardent
Praises of my poetry's belief.

Beloved, they are right!
Damn right.

Your absence keeps me company
Fills my emptiness with your essence
Rustling the hairs on my skin, giving me
The feel of your touch and kiss.

Your absence brings me company
In the words you scribble on virgin white
In the existence hidden in the horizon
After the letter Z and the space
Before the letter A.

I've found sanity in this madness
In all the words not in the Dictionary
In all the languages not spoken
In all the emptiness never filled.

Beloved, they would never understand
Never understand us
Us together!

No poem could ever match your poetry
You name all my Nouns
You give action to all my Verbs
You qualify all my Adjectives
And still you remained the nameless
With a million names,
The momentum of the moment,
The unqualified quality
That has been qualified unquantifiably.

My beloved, they would never know
Never know what only I know
That –

You're the mellow colours behind the sun rays
You're the hidden moon at noon
Heating the scalding sun
You're the water flowing under the desert sands
You're the thirst in the bosom of the sea.

Beloved, you're my madness.

Abubakar Othman

THERE IS METHOD IN YOUR MADNESS

My beloved, believe them
If they call you mad
For it takes one to know one,
And madness is a pleasure to treasure
Which only the mad know.

How long has it taken the sane world
To know the worth of madness!

Today the so-called civilized world
Imitate what was inimitable attributes
Of insanity, adorning the fashion of madness
As the dress code of modern celebrities.

The madman wears rags with bare buttocks
The celebrities wear torn and tanned jeans
Half way down below the anus,
The women dressed half naked
Like the madman, in skimpy dress
Dotted with holes and patches like the
Leftovers of termites.

Their Aunties, the oldies defying age
Fill their empty bra with sweet melon
Thrusting them at the men as breasts
And the randy dandies with their dildos
Dote on them to stir their stale desire
A delusional fantasy only madness can fathom.

The madman and the modern celebrities
All wear the same weird hairstyle
And walk with bare breasts and buttocks.

My beloved, ignore the lunatics
Who say you're a fanatic
Because you adore me with the ardent faith
Of your poetry's belief.
What can they tell you about religion
Hypocrites they are,
Preaching celibacy, practicing sodomy
Shouting peace, shooting bullets
In their catechism of debauchery.

You seek essence in the absence of presence
They seek affluence in the presence only
The essence of my absence fills your emptiness
With my invisible presence rustling
Through the hairs and nerves of your body
Giving you solace, giving you peace.
How can you compare the peace you dispense
In the realms of love
With the peace they destroy
In the name of Chrislam.

My beloved, believe them
If they call you mad
For the insane are the truly sane.
There is beauty in every madness
Which only the insane can see,
Ours is hidden in the
Complex simplicity of our language of love.

Habeebatu X!

TALES OF MAN

I

You were everything they warned me about
When you walked into my room – my heart
With the swagger of a man who dropped
The panties of the muses like a thunderbolt,
And you knew it.

You smashed through the walls of my vessel
With fire burning in your eyes, passion
Sending strong waves through my veins, desire
Till lust and longing stirred a volcano in me,
And you knew it.

You left hard liquor on your lips
Coated with strawberry taste and nectar,
And stirred my appetite till I was panting, for it
Then you feasted on my fountain,
And you knew it.

You held my life in your palms – my god
When you squeezed, my heart whined for you
When you let go, my heart yearned for more
Till I became a slave on my knees
Begging for salvation,
And by God, you knew it.

II

A thousand poems for you and still
    It feels I've not written anything
Do I turn your smiles into ink so that
I can pen the words on the parchment of my heart,
Do I strip my skin to let your soft caresses?
Reach deep into my flesh, moulding me afresh.

A million words later and still
I have not said anything of our secrets
Do I resonate with your 'I love yous'
So the resonance can reproduce the emotion.

Do I pull my heart out to the paper
So that it sees how wild that it beats
For you without the thought of death.

A billion tales of man later still
Yet you remain, the man – a man
The only man I wish to be a woman for
Just you. The man.

III

And there were moments
Looking at the stars when
I felt love for him suffocating
        - aweight on my chest
Making it impossible to breath.

Those moments where nothing
        Not even poetry or music
Could capture how it squeezed
        - painful, tight around my heart
                Making it impossible to beat.

I swear there were moments
        When I feared I was insane
Talking to winds about how
        He muffled my leaves and made me sing
The tale of this man to the Sahara winds.

To the sand dunes to the camels
        That left imprints on my mind
The tales of this man I whispered
        To fishes and sea weeds
To live forever in this water
        This man.

IV

As the sun slips under the blanket of sky
        I pull him closer to me
Tracing my hands over his skin
Straightening the corners of my favourite poem
        Swiping my tongue across his seams

Like makeshift glue keeping these sheaves together
As the sky undresses the moon in haste
I pull him closer still to me
Staring into his eyes in wonder
Memorizing the lines of my favourite poem
Pausing with each whiff of his breath
Like enjambments keeping these lines together.

As the stars giggle at the moon's chorus
I pull him closer still to me
Melding my skin with his
Hugging the parchment of my favourite poem
Tasting each drop of ink
Like whiskey keeping this poet drunk
On her favourite poem
As the sun slips under the blanked of sky
I tell the fading sun of this man
Who is my favourite poem.

Abubakar Othman

AND YOU KNEW IT

The seducers came to you as suitors
To lure you with their fathic words
And furtive ways, promising you
Their hearts of soot,
And you knew it.

I came to you a gallant Knight
Galloping on my Stallion of Passions,
Your elfin grin enticed me
Into the ambush of your arms,
And you knew it.

Your embrace around me was cloying
I surrendered my Knighthood
To be the Shepherd of your desires
My heart your lush land,
And you knew it.

Now listen, my elfish nymph
Before your delirious desires
Subdue my voice with lust:

I'm not the chivalrous knight
That masturbates on horseback
At the sight of a fair lady,
Nor am I a seducer
Searching for a lolita to lure.

I'm the gallant Knight to rescue fair ladies

From errant Knights on prowl,
I'm the shepherd of love
My flocks are antelopes of passions
Grazing in the lush land of my heart,
I ride on my stallion of desires
Keeping watch over them,
My hoofsteps make oases in their tracks.

II

The eclipse of the moon
Does not make the night too gloomy to smile
When the sun flashes its teeth at dawn,
Even at dusk the sun penetrates
The translucent walls of the night.

My dear *habibi*
You're the cheerful smile of dawn
That divests the lonely night of its gloom,
You're the radiance of day
That clears the cataract in the night's eyes
And now that the shepherd
Has found his studmare
I shall sing you madrigal songs
To urge your manicured feet
Through the quicksands of the desert
Taking you from the land of the pyramids
To the land of a million horses.

Yahabibi, **wushekindero**
(You are welcome),
Here I offer you dust powder
For your eye shadow
Dry wind for your wet lips
Soursweat for your perfume

And torrential heat for your bath –
The traditional wedding gifts of the desert.

Our hospitality is our identity
Let the hot sun blush your rosy cheeks
And the cold night hug your supple body
You will feel tonight the amorous tremors
Of love in the cloying embrace of harmattan
You will sleep tonight with open eyes
In the rhythmic embrace of your Knight.

III

This crowd is darker
Than the night behind this light
And the flutes, and the drums
And the stampede of these dancers
Impede my ears from the message
Of this smile spread like lip stick
On your lips.

How splendid you appear
In this crowd of blind spectators
And oblivious admirers
Stupefied by loose beauties
Wriggling cheap waists
In the wedding dance.

Let's sneak out of the crowd
And walk in the dark, step by step
Your soft voice in the silent night
Is sweeter than the beggars flutes
Your gentle steps on the dry grasses
Are soothing to my ears

Than the stampeding feet of these dancers.

I know is brighter here
These rivulets of light kindle
The embers of beauty ogling at me
In the hearth of your eyes,
But I will covet you more
In the private arms of the darkness
Beckoning us behind this light.

IV

Do not curse yourself for this prickish affair
Our union tonight is no accident,
There is no savagery in love
But wild desire
Every woman is a goddess
At the altar of love.

It's the trick of the hunter
To wear an antelope's head
And gambol with the gazelles in the bush
An amatory tactics of the cock and the hen.

Adam and Eve are no exception
Their contronym is temptation,
Our union tonight is no different
It started from the poet's grove,
The All Poets Network
Of the pyramid city of singing birds
Where I met my passionate goddess
Now a devout worshipper in the bed chamber
Of my Altar.

Habeebatu X!

YOUR LOVE HAS MADE ME INSANE

Roses whisper about me in hushed tones
  'She's definitely a one-petal-loose
  She has tried to pull nectar from
  These bees, Oh! how his love must sting'.

Clouds gossip about me in hushed strikes
  'She's definitely a one-drop free
  See how she tries to feed raindrops
  To the sky. Oh! how his love must drench'.

Stars talk about me at moonlight tales
  'She's definitely a one-shine empty
  Look at her trying to feed stardust
  To the sun. Oh! how his love must burn'.

Time discuss about me with the minutes
  'She's definitely a one-second-too late
  Watch how she tries to wind back time.
  Oh! how his love must drive her insane'.

Yes my love, your love has made me insane.

II
I wish I kissed your soul when our lips met
Instead of the sweet caress of your tongue
I wish I had tasted the fiery burn of your soul
And had my tongue branded a thief
I wish I had pulled your soul in tight embrace
Instead of just fiddling

With the treasures of your body
I wished these fingers had felt
The contours of your soul
Like it feels reading the braille,
Exploring your secrets.

I wish I had undressed you to the bones
Instead of running shaky fingers on your skin
I wish I had made love to the very soul
Of your body.

I wish I had trapped the sun within the sky
And made the night last longer than day,
I wish I had burned in it and made
My ashes the moon to keep us aglow
I wish I had done nothing
And done everything
For yet, the sun sailed home
That night that you made me a woman.

III
Like the fish in the river
I would immerse myself in your
Deeply, dearly, without reservation
Till I am you, in you, on you
All over you, conflated.

I would assume you, consume you
Completely, entirely, with no reprieve
Till I'm your definition, your identity,
I would be your lifeline –
Your breathing, your heartbeat, your blood
Without me you will be a fish washed ashore
Flapping, spasmodic, gasping for breathe.

IV

Like a fish at sea, I wan to be
Lost in this place full of you
Home-yet foreign land alike
Exploring all your nooks and crannies
Gliding through your hidden arteries
Tasting all of your flowing blood
Lost completely, wholly, entirely
Till Home is every drop that fasts
Like you
And time is every drop that touches me
And forever is every drop that is me.

V

Every drop of me exist for you
What is the sea without fishes
Every drop of you exists for me
What is the fish without the sea
For you, I am the sea and the fishes
The fishes and the sea
The purpose and the reason
In life and death
Your before and your after
Because in time, I've forgotten
If I exist for you or you exist for me.

Abubakar Othman

THE PICTURE IN MY EYES

The mirror does not remember things
It does not show history
Nor does it tell you time
Other than the present.

Therefore ignore the mirror
When it shows you how you look now
Does it know what you looked before.

You may look what the mirror says now
But I know what you looked
Before the mirror was invented.

That is the face I always see
When I look into your eyes
Which no mirror can mirror
Except the one in my eyes.

A broken heart is like a broken mirror
I'm not used to seeing myself
In a broken mirror.

MAKE ME YOURS

You've turned me to a nomad on my land
My pen races about its expanse
Finding lines long enough to bear
The words you have cursed me with.

Tonight I seek new pasture to graze on
These words of my ink flow like fountain
Come listen to its amorous sound
Before I let go, my beloved.

On this land of yours I shall no longer
Find the pasture for my heart to graze
On this land of yours my thirst shall not quench
On this land of yours solitude is my only companion.

But tonight my love, just for tonight
The stars must envy us in love
I'd find nourishment in the skin that clothes you
I'd strip you naked with my tongue
Till I taste the whole of you
I'd touch you strikingly,
Drawing sensuous lines on your body
From the dimples of your smiles
To the single dimple down below.

But beloved, the thought of being called 'his'
Of another voice whispering my name as 'his'
Grips me with grief,

The feel of his fingers drawing patterns on my body
Of his tongue finding patterns in my puzzles
Scatters me to pieces.

The thought of being his, my beloved
Breaks my heart.
But before I become 'his', just for tonight
Please my beloved make me yours
Before I become 'his'.

Abubakar Othman

ANSWER ME

If I tell you my lips are a pair of crucible
Burning with erotonic chemicals
Will you hold me by the waist and suck them?

If I tell you my heart is a burning hearth
With a bubbling cauldron of passions
Will you make musical notes of them
And dance the ballet with me?

If I tell you I'm the phallic mountain
Where desires grow with alchemical fecundity
Will you plant your pliant heart on it?

If I tell you I'm the silence you hear
Yodelling softly in your heart's ear
Will you defy words and say 'I love you'?

If all the world is a museum
And all your desires are artefacts
Will you let me be the curator?

If X! is equal to Y
Will you then say Y is me?

If you say 'yes' to all these
Then you are my ANSWER!

Habeebatu X!

JUST FOR YOU

If my heart slips through your fingers
One more time, do not panic
It would crawl back to you
Begging for a feel of your touch, one more time.

If my heart falls off the precipice
One more time, do not grieve
It would tumble and stumble down
Till the ground feels like home
With the delight of your first taste
Like a welcome kiss after a long day.

If my heart burns from your love
One more time, I'm afraid it won't be the last
It would burn and burn again
Till all science become fable
And the ashes sprinkle in time
Till moments are lost
And the particles would become yours again
And the push of your love would taste
Like brandy on a girl's night out –
Once again.

Because through time, through space,
Through memories, this heart would break,
Fall and burn for you
Just for you
Even when
I'm called 'his'.

Abubakar Othman

MATHEMATICAL SET

We are each other forever
Like the pair of compasses together,
One leg at the centre, the other at the outer
Together we make a perfect circle.

You're firmly fixed, no shaking
In the centre of my heart, yours forever,
My love keeps you steady, with serenading
While you orbit my milky way, with zest.

Together we make a perfect round
Each time you come around,
The centre is yours forever
To make the round whenever.

Habeebatu X!

DO NOT TELL ME TO WAIT

Tell me –
How do I get over my soulmate.

Do not tell me to recall his flows
He is flawless in all his ways,
Beautiful like the spread of the night sky
Dotted with starring stars

Do not tell me to love another in his place
This heart is a stubborn studmare
Unyielding to sweet words
Disobedient to harsh sticks
Impossible to persuade
Other than him.

Do not tell me time would heal
There are no wounds in this matter
Only consumptive love, a lingering passion
So I'm immune to time.

Do not tell me another would come
There's just no other
He is like the sun – singular
Of all the celestial bodies – brightest
Of all souls, he remains mine's mirror.

Do not tell me to pray
Like a demented worshipper
Lost in praises –
All I whisper is yaRabb
                    YaRabb
                              YaRabb.

Therefore, do not tell me to wait
I have waited from eon to eternity
My heartbeats counting the seconds
The minutes, the hours, the time ...

So just tell me
How do I get over him!

Abubakar Othman

DON'T YOU REMEMBER ME?

My soulmate, how can you get over it
The invincible though invisible fluke
Gambolling in your bloodcells,
Don't you remember me?

My name is X! + Y!
I was born that day you said to me
"I love you", in the year of the Reunion
On the great mountain of Passion.

Do you now remember ME?

The place of my birth is
The fleshy strip of land bordered by
The two quivering hills of mammary,
We often swarm together
In the cosy stream
Below the quivering hills.

Do you now remember ME

I used to slake my thirst
From the succulent springs of your hills
You once promised me
With your tongue in my ear
That you will always remember me.

Do you now remember ME

You gave me once a delightful picture
Which you can now see in the sensuous
Colours of my eyes,

You sang for me once a lustful serenade
Which I always cherish to remember
That which you can now hear
In the lyrical beats of my heartbeat –
Rhythmic, longing, asking:
How do I get over my soulmate?

Habeebatu X!

YOURS FOREVER

This lake shall not run dry
Have you ever heard of the sea
Gone empty, drained by the fishes?
I have not! And neither have those before me
And neither would those after me,
So is this lake that is yours forever
Yours to nourish
               Yours to cherish
To be home to you – a sanctuary
Then, now and forever
I am the sea,
               I am the lake
I am yours forever.

Abubakar Othman

I'M THE CLOUDS AROUND YOU

I'm the clouds your soar through
I caress your light feet with the
Rosebud tongue of cupid,
I'm the cherub in the sky
On whose wings you ride
To the realms of eternity
Where lies forever delight.

Together we shall live forever
Beyond the sun, beyond the moon
Where darkness shines brightly
In the incandescent fluorescence
Of our eyes.

Swim, swim, my love
Through the cloying clouds
Of my sovereign body
The spiritual vortex
Of our votive love.

Habeebatu X!

SALVATION

If religion is salvation
Then I've found paradise worshipping
At your Altar, feeling delirious
With amorous ecstasy from
The whiff of frankincense and musk
Of your sweaty body.

The soft moans and shrill shrieks
Of your pleas at the peak
Are like call to prayers, to devotion
And a devout worshipper I am
I spread you on the bed, a prayer mat
Taste the water of your mouth, a cleansing
Count the hairs on your chest, a prayer beads
Praying with insatiable desire, begging
Let the steam of your sweat
Purify this sinner
Sitting seething
On your belly bottom.

'Dear Lord, forgive this sinner'

Like the holy water of communion
I lick the sweats off your skin –
Salty. Tasty. Tempting...
Like the taunting temple of your navel
And the rod of paradise beneath it,
Filling me with its heat waves
Feeding me with its ambrosia
The sumptuous food of immortality

The amorous nectar of salvation.

'Dear Lord, grant me mercy'

And like a madone scared of light
I bury my face and find salvation
In darkness.

Othman/Habeebatu X!

POSTSCRIPT

And now the dearlogue is over
And the message is all over,
We need to keep a thermometer
To constantly read the temperature.
Love can sometimes wilt or wither
We must study it like the weather
To avoid going out in a raincoat
On a sunny day.

This love will never wither
And only us can ever measure
The inner temperature of the weather.
I'll always know when the kitchen is hot
And not to confuse it with the outside
weather
To avoid going out skimpy-scanty
On a cold rainy day.

OURS

FOREVER

You Came As a Thief,
But You Smiled!
So I Handed It Myself.

- NaseebaBabale

WHO IS HABEEBATU X!?

Habeebatu X! is a 22 year-old medical graduate who has found life in the pages of poetry and she remains tongue-tied anytime she's asked about herself.

How does it all start– this art of dropping stanzas?
It's like rainfall. Sometimes, it's heavy winds and raging storms. The muse gathers like clouds and demands to fall. And sometimes, it's light showers. I fixate on a prompt or image or word or phrase and the words start to piece together slowly and gently. So yes, it's like rainfall..

What purpose does poetry serve to you?
It's therapy for me. A safe place to pour the thoughts in my head and with imagery and creativity, I can hide my truths and secrets in plain sight.

Most of your poems are robustly romantic, why?
I love love.

You are seen as a social media poet, an Instagram poet, to be specific. Don't you think there is need for you to publish your works in literary magazines or even publish a book?
I think this image is one I created from ease and a reluctance to leave my comfort zone. But I'd in shaa Allah, look into publishing. And the fact that I'm so lazy and procrastinate a lot. But I'm working on something ☺

What can you say about Poetic Wednesdays?
I learnt about poetic Wednesday at about the time I expanded my circle of poetry friends and I find I am rather fascinated by the platform. I think they are doing something beautiful and

I've always wanted to be a member but that hasn't happened yet.

In most of your works ,there are hardly mention of 'harmattan' or 'dry season', only 'summer, winter, spring, etc'. Some people think this is wrong of an African writer. What's your take on that?
I think this may be because growing up as a reader, most of what I read were non-African books. I loved romance books and most were full of summer, winter and spring. But as I identify more with my roots and grow, I try to make conscious efforts to be more African.

Gender issues now trends across the globe and Africa in particular, how do you see the idea of feminism?
This is a very sensitive issue these days. And everybody hangs on to whatever someone says on the issue not to understand but to judge. But I'd say this; women need to be given a voice to talk about their problem as women without judgment.

If you are to take a 12-hour walk with any PW member into a desert without phone and internet, who would that be?
Aunty NaseebaBabale. She's my muse's lover.

Who are your best writers?
I don't read much of poetry. I read more of social media poetry and they are certain people I look up to and enjoy their works immensely like NaseebaBabale, MariyaSidi, Bedouin and 'a nagging voice tells me I'm forgetting someone else.' And of course, Umar Sidi – writing a collab with him would be amazing.

Favourite food and musician?
My food choices really depend on my mood. But music, my absolute favourites are Nicki Minaj and Lana del Rey (I see traces of LDR in my poems.)

What's your idea of a fine poem?
Good grammar. Proper spellings. Imagery. Metaphors.

You are one of the founders of a poetry movement, For the Love of Poetry, therefore you get to encounter a lot of young poets especially from the North here. So what can you say? Are the writers promising?
Yes, we are. Very promising. Everyday I am left in awe by the talent we have.

What's one surprising thing about you only a few know?
I love camels.

What do you do when free?
Sing really loud and dance really offbeat.

Advice to aspiring writers?
I have had the pleasure of meeting so many 'aspiring' writers like myself and I think the major advice I can give is for every writer to make a decision as to what they want and why they write. Decide whether you write to be better at it or if you do it for the social media fame and the 'wow's. The former would make you more open to corrections, to learning and makes you humble. While the former makes you believe you and your pen are supreme and that is bad. A poet who doesn't welcome criticisms with the same ado as compliments are one who is unwilling to grow. And read! Read! It's an excellent way to experience new things and grow your

vocabulary, and learn. You are only as good as you read. And you can't give what you don't have.

A CONVERSATION WITH ABUBAKAR OTHMAN

Othman Teaches African Literature and Creative writing
At the Department of English and Literary Studies, University of
Maiduguri

Could you tell us about growing up, your family?
*I had a suburban childhood, regimented by family tradition
and communal life. I was the second child in a family of ten
children born to the same mother, to the same father.
Although I was born and brought up in an agrarian village,
my father never took any one of us to the farm. We woke up
very early for the morning prayers; we attended the
neighbourhood mosque where my father was the Imam. We
use to have early morning breakfast prepared together with
that of our father who would carry his own to the farm. As he
set out to the farm, we also set out to the Qur'anic school,
carrying along with us our school bag and broom. The
Qur'anic school closed some minutes to 7.00 am to allow us
sprint to the primary school. We came home at 9 o'clock for
breakfast and closed from the primary school around 1 pm. By
2 O'clock we were already on our way to the Qur'anic school
for afternoon lesson, and by 4 pm we would leave for the
primary school for evening games. We come back home by 6
pm and immediately after the Magrib prayers and after
taking our evening meal, we would be rushing back to the
Qur'anic school for the night lesson. We close at 9.00 pm and
rush back home through the dark foot path hemmed by
grasses and shrubs, lit only by the fleeting light of the fireflies
and kept alive by the eerie lyrics of the crickets and sonorous
crooking of the frogs. We must go to bed latest by 10.00 pm.
So we had less than an hour to play at night and virtually no
time to play during the day except on weekends.*

When did you start writing?
I started scribbling lines of poetry right from the primary school, but I had good literature teachers at the secondary school, so I started writing consciously at that level for the school magazine.

As an academic teaching creative writing, in addition to courses in literature, has teaching affected your work?
Yes it has, but positively. Teaching creative writing keeps me writing as well, and teaching African poetry as a course has continued to enrich my knowledge of poetry giving me inspiration to write.

Suppose you're to make out a poet as they say out of a whole cloth, what attributes, temperaments and sensibilities would you give him or her?
I would dress him/her in a robe of many colours like the one Joseph wore. I would not make him meek like Joseph or naïve like Dolly Parton but sybaritic, resplendent and vivacious like Naette in Senghor's poem. I am primarily a romantic poet who sees beauty and hears sweet music even at the graveyard.

Have you ever considered writing prose, aside from critical essays?
During my past sojourn in politics and my recent stint with the law enforcement agency fighting economic crimes, I have gained so much experience that is too ugly for poetry and too cantankerous to the sublime passion of a romantic poet. I am currently capturing these experiences in a semi-autobiographical novel, while some of them I have already made them into short stories.

Does a writer perceive differently than other people? Do you think there is anything unique about the writer's eye?

Well, every individual has the ability to perceive, and we all perceive differently even as writers. However, writers being people with unique imaginative ability, are more profound in their perception, being capable of perceiving beyond the real to the surreal, that is, as we say of poets, they can see in the dark.

As a poet who deploys language in a different way, do you ever feel struck (or stuck) by the limitations of language?

Struck no! But stuck yes! As a poet, language has never been an adequate tool for the expression of sublime feelings; that is why the poet often resorts to the use of imagery, symbolism, abstraction, ellipsis, etc, as extrapolation of the imagination which words are often inadequate to transpose. Therefore, rather than be struck by the limitation of language, I feel elated going beyond words to express myself.

How do you work? Can you describe how you wrote your first drafts?

How do I work? I work normal according to the dictate of the work. But how I write, yes! I write ex-tempore, like a jolt, a tic or a tickle. I write on impulse. Once there is the excitement, the fascination, the temptation – that stimulus to do a thing, I respond spontaneously, almost ex-tempore, and a draft is done.

Do you have a specific time, may be a day, or a place for writing? Does it matter where you are?

As I said earlier, writing is spontaneous, especially poetry. But once the spontaneous reaction to the stimulus is done and the draft is born, then where you are matters in writing the final draft – a suitable environment with a commensurate frame of mind is essential, if not necessary.

What in your opinion is the most difficult aspect of writing?

To me, the most difficult aspect of writing is when to stop. For the poem you must dispose of it immediately your final draft is made, otherwise the emotion vegetates and you find yourself re-writing it again.

You have been writing for close to twenty years now, do you look over your past works with some or any sense of pleasure? Would you, if given the chance, change it?

Writing is sometimes determined by the mood of the moment, the effect of time and space. What may have pleased you to write at a given moment or circumstance may not please you to write in another moment or situation. Although literary ideas are transcendental, but they are also conditioned by time, place and milieu.

Is there anything that sticks in your mind as having been your greatest reward as a writer, and why?

I am not sure if there is reward for writing in the material sense of the word; may be the Nobel Prize and that is too far-fetched for me as an obscure writer on the fringe. However, writing is partly expurgatory, it is cathartic. Perhaps your reward is the catharsis – the expurgation of the suffocating feelings lurking in your heart or gambolling in your blood veins. However, there is something that sticks in my mind that gives me pleasure to remember. It was a letter written to me by a young college student somewhere in Riyom (Jos) appreciating my poems which I used to publish with the then

Sunday New Nigerian. She was pleading with me to teach her how to write and express her emotion the way I do, that was sometime in the late 1980s. I feel happy because I was able to impact positively on the mind of this young college girl, who I may be something of a role model to.

Let's talk about your poetry; your thoughts about it: do you have any primary imaginative concerns when you set out to write a poem?
My poetry is partly my personality – how I think, how I perceive issues and situations. My primary concern, however, is how to bring imagination to bear on reality – a creative representation or re-interpretation of reality. When I write, I am conscious of the basic reality and its common perception; I therefore want to deviate from the common perception as a mark of originality and individuality.

In writing a poem, what inspires that elusive first line?
The elusive first line, for poetry, is usually inspired by the muse; and that is one line or phrase or word that is difficult to change no matter how often you return to the draft (site). I cannot remember where I made that analogy between writing a poem and building a house, I talk too much in so many places, I've forgotten. But the analogy is instructive nevertheless. Writing a poem, like building a house requires planning and materials, and just as spontaneous as the urge to write is, so is the decision to build a house. But the process differs. In building, you are always sure of the bill of quantity, and as you build, you know where to place each block and how to fix every angle; in poetry, it is polyphonic, and what matters is the end.

What about revision? What part does revision play in the way you write – do you often get a poem in one go, so to speak, or do you work on draft after draft?
Revision plays a significant role in creative writing – the more you revise, the finer it becomes. However, in poetry, vigorous revision can vitiate the emotional strength of a poem and reduce its sublimity. Poetry may be creative but it is a creative or artistic truth. Sometimes you can write a poem at a go and be contented with it.

Do you have a concept of the reader?
No!

Are your writings directly autobiographical?
No!

What was the first book that meant something to you?
Alejo Carpentier's In the Kingdom of this World

How did it feel writing in a language that wasn't the one you'd grown up speaking?

It is challenging but exciting. I think in Fulfulde and write in English, it is a novelty indeed.

What would you recommend a poet study, especially a young one?
Because of the cacophony of contemporary Nigerian poetic voices, I would not recommend any to a young poet. I would have loved to because of the immediacy of their themes but they are confusing in style and careless with language. The second generation poets are appropriate. Tenure Ojaide is good, Niyi Osundare is exciting, Odia Ofeimun is inspiring; but reading older poets such as Gabriel Okara, J.P. Clark,

some poems of Soyinka is a sure way of mastering the techniques of good poetry.

How would you characterize the way your style has evolved over the many years you've been writing?
I would characterize it the same way with the course of a river. I started plainly, flowing freely, unencumbered by technicalities. But as I entered the middle course, I had carried along sediments of style and techniques that I am now conscious of and are slowing down my free flow of thought and purity of mind. Presently, I have acquired too much load of poetic techniques that I am now sluggish, meandering into various tributaries like the river at its final stage.

You are engaged in different, often difficult activities and vocations: teaching, writing, you worked as a commissioner, a special adviser, director-general in your home state, Adamawa, as well as a Chief of Staff with the Economic and Financial Crime Commission (EFCC). How do you reconcile the rigours of what must be conflicting, even demanding enterprises?
The responsibilities are streamlined. Teaching is my permanent job, punctuated by writing as an essential component of literature. As a teacher of literature, you need exposure; you need to experience different phases and facets of life and society. It makes you a better teacher of life which literature is all about. It gives you a wider vista for writing. While doing those other jobs away from my teaching profession I was able to travel to virtually all African countries, and to most of the European nations. I have met people, I have seen places, and I have come into physical contact with many places that hitherto I only heard about them in novels, plays and poems. This knowledge enriches my

work as a lecturer, and empowers me to be more imaginative in my creative writing.

Printed in the United States
By Bookmasters